PRINCEWILL LAGANG

The Impact of Technology on Relationships

First published by PRINCEWILL LAGANG 2023

Copyright © 2023 by Princewill Lagang

All rights reserved. No part of this publication may be reproduced, stored or transmitted in any form or by any means, electronic, mechanical, photocopying, recording, scanning, or otherwise without written permission from the publisher. It is illegal to copy this book, post it to a website, or distribute it by any other means without permission.

Princewill Lagang asserts the moral right to be identified as the author of this work.

First edition

This book was professionally typeset on Reedsy.
Find out more at reedsy.com

Contents

1 Introduction — 1
2 The Digital Connection — 4
3 Balancing Online and Offline Lives — 7
4 The Social Media Effect — 10
5 Dating in the Digital Age — 13
6 Long-Distance Relationships in a Tech-Savvy World — 16
7 Sexting, Privacy, and Consent — 19
8 Communication Challenges — 22
9 Digital Distractions and Quality Time — 25
10 Technology's Role in Conflict and Resolution — 28
11 Parenting in the Digital Age — 31
12 Cultivating a Healthy Tech-Relationship Balance — 34

1

Introduction

In the era of rapid technological advancement, the landscape of human relationships has undergone a profound transformation. This chapter aims to introduce the central theme of how technology's pervasive presence has significantly shaped and reshaped the dynamics of relationships in the modern world. As we navigate this digital age, understanding the complex interplay between technology and human connections becomes imperative.

Section 1: The Technological Revolution

The opening section sets the stage by highlighting the unprecedented speed at which technology has infiltrated every aspect of our lives. From smartphones that serve as constant companions to the algorithms that tailor our online experiences, technology is omnipresent. This section underscores how these advancements have extended their influence to the very core of our relationships, ushering in a new era where virtual interactions are as significant as physical ones.

Section 2: The Dichotomy of Connection and Disconnection

In this section, the chapter delves into the dichotomy that technology introduces—simultaneously fostering connections while fueling disconnections. Social media platforms promise to bridge geographical gaps, yet paradoxically can lead to feelings of isolation and inadequacy. The allure of constant communication clashes with the erosion of genuine face-to-face conversations. This section aims to dissect these contradictory effects, offering insight into the psychological toll of such a paradox.

Section 3: Redefining Relationship Norms

The third section explores how technology has redefined traditional relationship norms. Online dating apps have revolutionized how people meet and form romantic connections, challenging the conventions of courtship. Long-distance relationships have found newfound viability through video calls and instant messaging, but also introduce unique challenges. The rise of virtual friendships blurs the line between real and digital connections, prompting questions about authenticity and intimacy.

Section 4: Challenges and Complexities

The final section of the chapter delves into the challenges and complexities that arise from the intersection of technology and relationships. Trust issues may stem from the ease of maintaining secret online identities, while miscommunication can arise from the absence of non-verbal cues in text-based communication. The pressures of projecting an idealized self on social media platforms can strain relationships as authenticity takes a backseat.

Conclusion

Chapter 1 concludes by highlighting the importance of understanding technology's role in relationships. The chapter serves as a stepping stone for

INTRODUCTION

the subsequent sections, each of which will delve deeper into specific aspects of this intricate relationship between technology and human connections. By examining the transformative impact of technology, this work aims to provide a comprehensive understanding of the challenges and opportunities it presents for modern relationships.

Remember, this is just an outline for Chapter 1. You can expand on each section to create a detailed and engaging introduction for your work.

2

The Digital Connection

In an age defined by instantaneous communication, the digital landscape has transformed how individuals interact and connect with each other. This chapter delves into the multifaceted revolution of communication brought about by technology, examining its far-reaching effects on modern relationships.

Section 1: A Revolution in Communication

This section provides an overview of how technology has revolutionized communication, transcending geographical boundaries and temporal limitations. The proliferation of messaging apps, social media platforms, and video conferencing tools has not only accelerated the exchange of information but also redefined the very nature of conversation. The rapidity and accessibility of digital communication have shaped new norms and expectations for staying connected.

Section 2: The Positive Effects of Instant Connectivity

In this section, the chapter explores the positive impacts of instant connectivity on relationships. Digital communication has enabled real-time connection irrespective of physical distance, strengthening connections between loved ones separated by oceans. It has allowed families to bridge time zones and share moments as if they were together. Additionally, couples in long-distance relationships benefit from virtual intimacy, fostering emotional closeness despite being physically apart.

Section 3: The Dark Side of Hyperconnectivity

Section 3 delves into the negative consequences of hyperconnectivity within relationships. While technology facilitates constant interaction, it can lead to compulsive behaviors, where individuals feel pressured to respond immediately. This pressure can strain relationships, causing misunderstandings when responses are not immediate. Furthermore, the illusion of connection through digital platforms can sometimes replace deeper face-to-face conversations, resulting in shallow interactions and a diminished sense of emotional closeness.

Section 4: Communication Overload and Misinterpretation

This section discusses the concept of communication overload, where the abundance of communication channels can overwhelm individuals. Frequent notifications, messages, and updates can lead to information fatigue, diminishing the quality of interactions. Moreover, the absence of non-verbal cues in digital communication can lead to misinterpretation and misunderstandings. Tone, intent, and emotions can be misconstrued in text-based conversations, potentially causing conflicts.

Section 5: Striking a Balance

The final section of this chapter focuses on the importance of striking a balance between digital and physical communication. It explores strategies for managing the digital connection to enhance rather than hinder relationships. This section emphasizes the significance of mindful communication, setting boundaries to prevent burnout, and carving out time for meaningful in-person interactions.

Conclusion

Chapter 2 concludes by highlighting the intricate interplay between technology and communication within relationships. It underscores the need for a nuanced approach, where technology serves as a tool for connection rather than a replacement for genuine interactions. By acknowledging both the advantages and pitfalls of the digital connection, individuals can navigate this new terrain with greater awareness and intentionality.

3

Balancing Online and Offline Lives

In a world where digital interactions have become integral to daily life, maintaining a harmonious equilibrium between virtual and physical interactions is paramount. This chapter delves into the complex task of striking a balance between the digital realm and the real world within the context of relationships.

Section 1: The Digital Invasion into Personal Space

This section delves into the challenges posed by the encroachment of digital devices and platforms into personal space. It examines how the constant availability of technology can blur the boundaries between work, personal time, and relationships. The section highlights the need to address this intrusion to foster healthier and more fulfilling connections.

Section 2: The Art of Unplugging

Section 2 explores the concept of "unplugging" as a means to reclaim quality time in relationships. It discusses the benefits of disconnecting from screens and devices periodically to engage in authentic face-to-face interactions. The section provides insights into the positive impact of setting designated "unplugged" times, allowing couples to be fully present with each other.

Section 3: Strategies for Quality Time Together

This section delves into practical strategies for spending quality time together without the distractions of technology. It explores activities that encourage engagement, intimacy, and meaningful conversations. From outdoor adventures to shared hobbies, the section offers a range of ideas to help couples forge deeper connections beyond the virtual realm.

Section 4: Mindful Digital Engagement

In this section, the chapter discusses the concept of mindful digital engagement. It emphasizes the importance of being present even during virtual interactions. The section explores how being fully engaged during video calls or text conversations can enhance the quality of the connection, making up for the lack of physical presence.

Section 5: Creating Digital-Free Zones

Section 5 highlights the significance of creating designated spaces that are free from digital distractions. It suggests carving out areas in homes where technology is intentionally limited, fostering an environment conducive to authentic interactions. The section also discusses how such spaces can serve as a refuge from the constant noise of notifications.

Conclusion

Chapter 3 concludes by emphasizing that the quest for balance between online and offline lives is an ongoing journey that requires conscious effort. It underscores the importance of cultivating self-awareness about technology usage and its impact on relationships. By incorporating strategies to unplug, spend quality time together, and engage mindfully, couples can navigate the digital landscape while preserving the intimacy and authenticity that characterize meaningful connections.

4

The Social Media Effect

The proliferation of social media platforms has introduced a new layer of complexity to relationships, influencing how individuals perceive themselves and each other. This chapter delves into the multifaceted impact of social media on self-esteem, jealousy, trust, and provides strategies for maintaining a healthy online presence as a couple.

Section 1: Crafting the Perfect Image

This section explores how social media encourages the curation of carefully crafted images and narratives. It discusses how individuals often present an idealized version of their lives, which can lead to unrealistic comparisons and diminished self-esteem. The section highlights the importance of recognizing these curated representations for what they are and promoting self-acceptance.

Section 2: Jealousy in the Age of Comparison

In this section, the chapter examines how social media can amplify feelings of jealousy and insecurity. The constant exposure to others' seemingly flawless lives can lead to envy and self-doubt. The section delves into the psychological underpinnings of jealousy in the digital age and offers strategies for managing these emotions within relationships.

Section 3: Navigating Trust Issues

Section 3 delves into the impact of social media on trust within relationships. The prevalence of online interactions, from liking posts to connecting with new people, can sometimes lead to mistrust. The section discusses how open communication and setting boundaries can help build and maintain trust in the face of these challenges.

Section 4: Strategies for Healthy Social Media Use

This section offers practical strategies for couples to navigate social media in a healthy and constructive manner. It discusses the benefits of open communication about online activity and mutual support in dealing with the emotional effects of social media. The section also explores the concept of "digital detox" and setting limits on screen time.

Section 5: Fostering Authentic Connections Online

In this final section, the chapter focuses on the potential for fostering authentic connections on social media. It discusses how couples can leverage technology to share genuine moments and celebrate their relationship milestones. The section emphasizes the value of using social media as a platform for positive interactions and reaffirming their connection.

Conclusion

Chapter 4 concludes by emphasizing the need for mindfulness in social media usage and its impact on relationships. It underscores that while social media can present challenges, it also offers opportunities for couples to strengthen their bonds and express their love and support. By recognizing the effects of social media on self-esteem, jealousy, and trust, couples can proactively navigate this digital landscape while prioritizing the health of their relationship.

5

Dating in the Digital Age

The advent of technology has revolutionized the way individuals approach dating and finding romantic partners. This chapter explores the evolution of dating apps and online matchmaking, delving into the advantages and challenges of navigating the world of romance through digital platforms.

Section 1: The Rise of Online Matchmaking

This section traces the evolution of dating from traditional methods to the digital landscape. It highlights how dating apps and online matchmaking platforms have reshaped the way people meet potential partners. The section discusses how algorithms and compatibility metrics have come to replace more traditional methods of matchmaking.

Section 2: The Advantages of Digital Dating

In this section, the chapter examines the advantages of using technology to find romantic connections. It discusses how dating apps increase the pool of potential partners, enabling individuals to meet people they might not have crossed paths with otherwise. The section also explores the convenience and efficiency of online dating, allowing users to connect at their own pace and on their own terms.

Section 3: The Challenges of Virtual Connections

Section 3 delves into the challenges that come with forming relationships through digital means. It discusses how the digital dating landscape can sometimes lead to shallow interactions and surface-level connections. The section also explores the phenomenon of "ghosting" and the lack of accountability that can sometimes arise in virtual interactions.

Section 4: Navigating Authenticity and Deception

This section addresses the issue of authenticity and deception in online dating. It discusses the potential for users to present idealized versions of themselves, which can lead to disappointment and mistrust when expectations are not met. The section offers strategies for navigating these challenges and promoting genuine connections.

Section 5: Balancing Virtual and Real-Life Interactions

In this final section, the chapter explores the importance of striking a balance between virtual and real-life interactions within the context of online dating. It discusses the value of transitioning from virtual conversations to in-person meetings to foster deeper connections. The section also emphasizes the significance of maintaining authenticity both online and offline.

Conclusion

Chapter 5 concludes by underscoring the transformative impact of technology on the dating landscape. It emphasizes that while digital platforms offer unprecedented opportunities to connect with potential partners, they also present unique challenges. By approaching online dating with intentionality, open communication, and a willingness to bridge the gap between virtual and real-life interactions, individuals can navigate the complexities of dating in the digital age and forge meaningful romantic connections.

6

Long-Distance Relationships in a Tech-Savvy World

Long-distance relationships have been redefined by the technological advancements that enable constant connection across vast distances. This chapter delves into the transformative impact of technology on long-distance relationships, exploring the ways in which digital tools can be leveraged to maintain connection and intimacy despite geographical separation.

Section 1: Redefining Long-Distance Relationships

This section examines how technology has redefined the landscape of long-distance relationships. It discusses how video calls, instant messaging, and virtual intimacy have allowed couples to bridge the gap of physical separation. The section explores how the ability to see and hear a partner in real time has transformed the way individuals maintain relationships across distance.

Section 2: Nurturing Connection Through Virtual Interaction

In this section, the chapter delves into the strategies for maintaining connection and intimacy through virtual interactions. It discusses the importance of regular video calls and how they enable couples to share experiences despite being apart. The section also explores the potential for shared online activities, such as watching movies or playing games, to create a sense of togetherness.

Section 3: The Challenges of Absence and Trust

Section 3 addresses the challenges that long-distance relationships still face despite technological advancements. It discusses the emotional toll of physical absence and the potential for feelings of loneliness and insecurity. The section also explores how technology can sometimes introduce challenges related to trust, as partners may not be physically present to provide reassurance.

Section 4: Overcoming Miscommunication and Time Zones

This section delves into the potential for miscommunication and time zone differences to affect long-distance relationships. It discusses how the lack of non-verbal cues in digital communication can lead to misunderstandings and conflict. The section also offers strategies for effective communication across time zones, emphasizing the importance of patience and understanding.

Section 5: Creating Rituals and Shared Experiences

In this final section, the chapter discusses the significance of creating rituals and shared experiences to maintain intimacy in long-distance relationships. It explores how technology can facilitate activities like virtual date nights, joint playlists, or online cooking sessions, fostering a sense of connection and shared moments.

Conclusion

Chapter 6 concludes by highlighting the potential of technology to transform the dynamics of long-distance relationships. It emphasizes that while geographical separation poses challenges, the tools at our disposal enable couples to navigate these challenges with greater ease. By leveraging technology to nurture connection, trust, and intimacy, individuals can build resilient and fulfilling relationships across distances in this tech-savvy world.

7

Sexting, Privacy, and Consent

The digital age has introduced new dimensions to intimacy, with sexting becoming a prevalent form of connection for many couples. This chapter explores the implications of digital intimacy, consent, and the importance of navigating privacy concerns in the modern relationship landscape.

Section 1: The Landscape of Digital Intimacy

This section sets the stage by discussing the emergence of digital intimacy and how technology has reshaped how couples express affection and desire. It examines how sexting and sharing explicit content have become part of romantic interactions, exploring both the allure and potential risks associated with this form of expression.

Section 2: Consent in the Digital Realm

In this section, the chapter delves into the critical topic of consent within the context of digital interactions. It examines how consent applies to the sharing of intimate content and discusses the importance of mutual understanding, communication, and enthusiastic agreement. The section highlights the potential consequences of sharing explicit content without explicit consent.

Section 3: Navigating Privacy Concerns

Section 3 explores the challenges of maintaining privacy in a digital era. It discusses the risks associated with sharing intimate content, including the potential for leaks, hacks, or unintended recipients. The section offers strategies for couples to navigate privacy concerns, including discussions about boundaries, trust, and the importance of using secure communication platforms.

Section 4: Building Trust in Digital Intimacy

This section emphasizes the role of trust in digital intimacy. It discusses how trust is the foundation for sharing intimate content and engaging in sexting. The section explores how open communication, respecting boundaries, and setting clear expectations contribute to a sense of security and trust within the relationship.

Section 5: Managing the Digital Legacy

In this final section, the chapter discusses the concept of managing the digital legacy of intimate content. It explores the importance of considering the long-term implications of sharing explicit content, especially in the event of a breakup. The section offers guidance on how to approach the conversation about what happens to shared content should the relationship end.

Conclusion

Chapter 7 concludes by emphasizing the multifaceted nature of digital intimacy, consent, and privacy. It underscores the importance of open communication, mutual respect, and understanding in navigating these complexities. By approaching digital intimacy with care, ensuring enthusiastic consent, and actively working to protect privacy, couples can navigate the digital landscape while fostering trust, respect, and authenticity in their relationships.

8

Communication Challenges

As technology shapes the way we communicate, new challenges and complexities arise in maintaining clear and meaningful interactions. This chapter delves into the various ways miscommunication and misunderstandings can occur in digital conversations and offers strategies for fostering effective communication in the age of technology.

Section 1: The Nuances of Digital Communication

This section examines the nuances that distinguish digital communication from face-to-face interactions. It discusses the absence of non-verbal cues, tone, and context that can lead to misinterpretation and misunderstanding. The section highlights the need to recognize these differences and their potential impact on relationship dynamics.

Section 2: The Pitfalls of Text-Based Conversations

In this section, the chapter explores the challenges presented by text-based conversations. It discusses how written messages can sometimes lack the depth and clarity of in-person conversations. The section also addresses the potential for messages to be misconstrued due to their brevity or ambiguity.

Section 3: Emojis and Visual Language

Section 3 delves into the role of emojis and visual cues in digital communication. It discusses how these elements can enhance text-based conversations by conveying emotions and intent. The section emphasizes the importance of using emojis mindfully to avoid overreliance and to ensure that messages are received as intended.

Section 4: Active Listening in Virtual Conversations

This section examines the concept of active listening in the context of virtual conversations. It discusses how distractions, multitasking, and the rapid pace of digital communication can hinder active listening. The section offers strategies for being present and attentive during online interactions to foster deeper understanding.

Section 5: Strategies for Effective Communication

In this final section, the chapter offers practical strategies for effective communication in the digital age. It explores the importance of clear and concise language, using context to provide clarity, and seeking clarification when messages are ambiguous. The section also discusses the value of scheduling regular video calls to engage in more comprehensive conversations.

Conclusion

Chapter 8 concludes by underlining the significance of communication in maintaining healthy relationships within the technology-driven landscape. It highlights that while digital communication poses challenges, it also offers opportunities for growth and understanding. By acknowledging the limitations, employing strategies for effective communication, and fostering active engagement, couples can navigate the communication challenges of the digital age while deepening their connections.

9

Digital Distractions and Quality Time

In a world buzzing with digital distractions, the ability to carve out undistracted quality time has become a challenge for many couples. This chapter delves into the impact of technology's intrusion on shared moments and offers techniques for fostering genuine connections amidst the digital noise.

Section 1: The Erosion of Quality Time

This section examines how technology distractions have led to the erosion of quality time in relationships. It discusses how the constant presence of smartphones, notifications, and online engagements can hinder meaningful interactions and contribute to a sense of detachment.

Section 2: The "Always On" Culture

In this section, the chapter explores the concept of the "always on" culture, where individuals are perpetually connected to their devices. It discusses the impact of this culture on relationships, including the diminished ability to fully engage in real-time interactions without the pull of digital diversions.

Section 3: Strategies for Undistracted Moments

Section 3 delves into practical strategies for prioritizing undistracted moments within relationships. It discusses the value of establishing digital-free zones, such as during meals or before bedtime, to foster deeper connections. The section also explores the concept of "digital detox" periods where devices are intentionally put aside to engage in meaningful activities.

Section 4: Mindful Presence in Shared Activities

This section emphasizes the importance of mindful presence during shared activities. It discusses how engaging in activities together can strengthen bonds, provided that both partners are fully invested in the experience. The section offers techniques for minimizing distractions and immersing oneself in the moment.

Section 5: Reclaiming Quality Conversations

In this final section, the chapter focuses on the art of quality conversations. It discusses the impact of technology on conversation dynamics and offers strategies for fostering meaningful dialogues. The section emphasizes active listening, asking open-ended questions, and creating an environment conducive to genuine exchange.

Conclusion

Chapter 9 concludes by highlighting the significance of undistracted quality time in maintaining healthy relationships. It underscores the necessity of setting boundaries with technology to allow for genuine connections. By implementing strategies to combat digital distractions, couples can reclaim the joy of spending focused and meaningful time together, cultivating bonds that transcend the digital realm.

10

Technology's Role in Conflict and Resolution

Technology's omnipresence has introduced a new dimension to conflicts within relationships. This chapter explores the ways in which technology can amplify conflicts and also offers insights into how digital tools can be harnessed for effective problem-solving and reconciliation.

Section 1: Amplification of Conflicts Through Technology

This section delves into how technology can amplify conflicts within relationships. It discusses how misunderstandings through digital communication can escalate due to the lack of non-verbal cues and tone. The section examines how impulsive messages sent in the heat of the moment can worsen conflicts.

Section 2: Digital Communication's Coldness

In this section, the chapter examines the potential for digital communication to lack the warmth and empathy present in face-to-face interactions. It discusses how written messages can sometimes appear distant and unfeeling, leading to further emotional disconnect during conflicts.

Section 3: Leveraging Technology for Resolution

Section 3 explores how technology can be harnessed as a tool for conflict resolution within relationships. It discusses the value of taking a pause during conflicts to cool down before engaging in digital communication. The section also explores the potential for using video calls to engage in more meaningful discussions.

Section 4: Virtual Problem-Solving Tools

This section focuses on the digital tools that can aid in problem-solving and reconciliation. It discusses the potential for collaborative apps that allow couples to discuss issues, set goals, and track progress. The section explores the value of technology in facilitating structured discussions that lead to resolutions.

Section 5: Reconciliation and Moving Forward

In this final section, the chapter discusses the role of technology in reconciliation and moving forward after conflicts. It explores the potential for using virtual spaces to share apologies, express remorse, and reaffirm commitment to the relationship. The section also underscores the importance of leveraging technology to rebuild trust.

Conclusion

Chapter 10 concludes by underscoring the dual nature of technology's impact on conflicts and resolution. While it can exacerbate misunderstandings, it also offers tools for effective problem-solving and reconciliation. By recognizing the pitfalls and potentials of technology, couples can navigate conflicts with greater awareness, fostering healthier communication and ultimately deepening their connection.

11

Parenting in the Digital Age

Raising children in the digital age presents a unique set of challenges and opportunities. This chapter delves into the complexities of parenting with technology's pervasive presence, exploring the impacts of digital devices on children and offering strategies for fostering healthy tech habits.

Section 1: The New Landscape of Childhood

This section examines the changing landscape of childhood in the digital age. It discusses how children are exposed to technology from an early age and explores the potential benefits and risks associated with their interactions with digital devices.

Section 2: Balancing Screen Time and Real Experiences

In this section, the chapter delves into the challenge of balancing screen time and real-life experiences. It discusses the potential for excessive screen time to impact children's development, from social skills to cognitive growth. The section emphasizes the importance of setting boundaries to ensure a well-rounded childhood.

Section 3: Navigating Online Safety

Section 3 addresses the critical topic of online safety for children. It discusses the risks associated with unsupervised internet access and explores strategies for protecting children from inappropriate content, cyberbullying, and online predators. The section highlights the significance of open communication about online interactions.

Section 4: Modeling Healthy Tech Habits

This section discusses the role of parents in modeling healthy tech habits for their children. It examines the potential impact of parental tech usage on children's behavior and explores the value of setting a positive example by prioritizing face-to-face interactions and designated tech-free times.

Section 5: Fostering Digital Literacy and Balance

In this final section, the chapter explores strategies for fostering digital literacy and balance in children's technology usage. It discusses the importance of teaching children critical thinking skills, responsible online behavior, and time management. The section offers ideas for incorporating educational tech activities that align with children's interests and developmental stages.

Conclusion

Chapter 11 concludes by underscoring the importance of proactive parenting in the digital age. It emphasizes the need for a balanced approach that harnesses the benefits of technology while safeguarding children's well-being. By fostering open communication, setting boundaries, and promoting healthy tech habits, parents can guide their children to navigate the digital landscape with mindfulness and resilience.

12

Cultivating a Healthy Tech-Relationship Balance

In the final chapter, we reflect on the journey of exploring technology's influence on relationships and delve into strategies for achieving a harmonious balance between technology and human connections.

Section 1: Reflecting on Insights

This section begins by summarizing the key insights gathered throughout the book. It revisits the various ways technology has impacted relationships, from reshaping communication dynamics to introducing new challenges and opportunities. The section prompts readers to reflect on their own experiences and recognize the evolving role of technology in their lives.

Section 2: The Power of Intentional Engagement

In this section, the chapter emphasizes the significance of intentional engagement with technology. It discusses the importance of setting intentions, being mindful of usage patterns, and recognizing when technology enhances or hinders meaningful interactions. The section explores how conscious choices can lead to healthier tech-relationship dynamics.

Section 3: Strategies for Balance

Section 3 delves into actionable strategies for achieving a healthy tech-relationship balance. It revisits the various themes explored in earlier chapters, including managing digital distractions, fostering communication, and setting boundaries. The section provides a concise guide for readers to implement these strategies in their own relationships.

Section 4: Nurturing Connection Amidst Technology

This section emphasizes the value of nurturing genuine connections amidst the digital noise. It discusses how meaningful relationships are built on shared experiences, authentic conversations, and emotional intimacy. The section underscores the importance of prioritizing face-to-face interactions and using technology as a tool to enhance, not replace, these connections.

Section 5: Embracing Technology's Evolution

In this final section, the chapter explores the concept of embracing technology's ongoing evolution. It discusses the ever-changing nature of digital advancements and how staying adaptable can help individuals and couples navigate future challenges and opportunities.

Conclusion

Chapter 12 concludes by summarizing the overarching message of the book: that technology's impact on relationships is multifaceted and requires intentional management. It underscores the importance of cultivating a healthy tech-relationship balance by being aware of the pitfalls and potentials of technology. By fostering mindful engagement, open communication, and prioritizing genuine connections, readers can navigate the digital landscape while nurturing meaningful, lasting relationships.

Conclusion: Navigating Relationships in the Digital Age

In a world where technology has seamlessly woven itself into the fabric of our lives, the landscape of relationships has undergone a profound transformation. Throughout this journey, we have explored the multifaceted impact of technology on human connections, delving into its potential to both enrich and challenge the dynamics that define our relationships.

From the digital communication revolution to the evolution of dating, the challenges of long-distance connections, and the complexities of parenting in the digital age, we have uncovered the intricate interplay between technology and relationships. We have examined how virtual interactions can enhance intimacy or lead to misunderstandings, how online platforms redefine courtship norms, and how digital tools can either bridge or widen the gaps between loved ones separated by distance.

Our exploration has revealed that the role of technology in relationships is not one-dimensional. It is a realm of possibilities, offering avenues for deepening connections, sparking new romances, and fostering growth. Yet, it also brings with it a range of challenges, from privacy concerns to communication breakdowns, that we must navigate with thoughtfulness and intention.

As we conclude this journey, we encourage you, the reader, to approach technology use mindfully and with open communication. Recognize that while technology can facilitate connections, it requires your active engagement to ensure those connections remain genuine and meaningful. Set boundaries that protect the sanctity of your relationships, prioritize in-person interactions, and use technology as a tool to enhance your connections rather than replace them.

In this dynamic landscape, let this book serve as a guide for embracing technology's potential while navigating its pitfalls. By fostering a healthy balance between the digital and physical realms, and by approaching technology with awareness, empathy, and a commitment to communication, you can cultivate relationships that thrive in the digital age and beyond.

www.ingramcontent.com/pod-product-compliance
Lightning Source LLC
LaVergne TN
LVHW010441070526
838199LV00066B/6119